Getting Away

A simple guide to moving to the countryside

By Arthur Kundell

Introduction

Have you ever looked around your cramped apartment and thought about moving away from it all? Driven from your suburban lot to the towering office block and wondered where your morning has gone? Stepped outside into peak hour traffic and wished for clean air and a few trees?

This book was written for those who are looking for more than their city life, those who are interested in moving away to the fresh air and wide-open spaces of the countryside. This can take many different forms – you may be looking for a small homestead in the mountains, a farming property in an agricultural region, a house in a small town. But all these dreams have a common desire, a wish for fewer people and more nature.

But how do you go about taking the step, turning your dreams into reality? It's a big change and one which requires planning – you need to know what is ahead of you, both the good and the bad.

That's where this book comes in. Easy to read and full of succinct advice, it gives you an overview of the main points which will come up before, during, and after your move to the countryside. With helpful hints to avoid the typical newbie mistakes, it's required reading for any who want to make the jump.

Each chapter focuses on a separate part of the process:

- **Part one** focuses on whether you *really* want to move. We look at the major advantages and disadvantages of living in the countryside as compared to the city, and provide a handy checklist to help decide if you've got the right mentality in place (page 10)

- **Part two** looks at finding a new home. The perfect home is of course very dependent on what you want, but we offer a number of helpful tips on things which you should keep in mind (page 21)

- **Part three** covers getting used to your new home and avoiding the typical newcomer mistakes. This includes things such as understanding why the town should be enjoyed on its own merits or accepting that you won't immediately be the centre of the town life (page 28)

- **Part four** looks at making friends, how to make a good first impression, become more than just 'the newcomer', and how to give back to the region (page 37)

- **Part five** involves integration, the ways you should act and the local knowledge you should keep an eye out for in order to truly become part of the community (page 49)

- **Part six** is all about gossip, one of the top pastimes in any rural area. We look at a few sanity-saving measures to keep your private life out of the gossip network (page 58)

- **Part seven** is there to help you during that moment when you feel lonely or bored in your new life. We offer tips on widening your circle of friends, taking up new hobbies, or getting out of town and trying something new (page 65)

- The **Appendix** offers a handy checklist for those who are about to move homes. It won't make the move stress-free but it will certainly save you a few handfuls of hair (page 75)

Still interested in escaping to the open fields and green forests? Then read on.

Table of contents

1. Do you really want to move?

The first big question is, naturally enough, are you *really* sure that you want to move to the countryside? It's a giant upheaval in your entire life, so you want to be very, very sure that it is the right thing to do *before* you do it.

As with anything, there are a number of pluses and minuses involved in the decision to move to a regional area or small town. The pluses include more space, cleaner environment, lower crime, cheaper living costs, and a better place for the children to grow up. The minuses include the limited infrastructure, the mental adjustment, the small-town attitudes, and the fact that the children will eventually grow up and leave. You'll need to weigh all of these factors when you are making your final decision.

So, let's have a look at these factors in a bit more detail. The following sections will go into the most common pluses and minuses, as well as following up with a checklist to see if you are mentally prepared for the rural lifestyle.

Plus points

There are a number of reasons which draw people from the large city into the smaller towns and villages of the countryside. Many of these are related to lifestyle and relaxation, in particular:

- More space to live
- A cleaner environment
- Lower crime rates
- Cheaper living costs
- Better lives for their family and children

Let's cover these in a bit more depth...

More space

Your average city is crowded, with many people living in a comparatively small area. Even the most spread-out of cities will have this same crowding problem, it is, after all, the definition of a city. The residents live in small apartments, townhouses, old buildings from decades ago and newly built high-rises where you are lucky to have a shower and a bathtub. There is a lack of space that pushes everyone together, always aware of your neighbours and always surrounded by the mass of humanity.

For many of us this is simply too much, we need our space, our open skies and our spread-out populations. Often families with children need that extra space – they need another bedroom or two, perhaps a living room to fit everyone in, a big garden to run around in. The sort of place where you can really stretch your arms and enjoy the room.

This is where the small towns are at their best. They are usually surrounded by plenty of land, with relatively few inhabitants to fill up the blocks. Small towns and the even more spread-out rural regions provide each resident with the free space which they are looking for. You will never find a block with space for a pool, garden, and a chicken or two in a major city (unless you are really quite amazingly rich). But in the country this is entirely possible, often for a surprisingly affordable cost. If your heartfelt dream is to enjoy the wind rushing through the trees on your block, or to watch the sunset from a quiet hillside porch, then the countryside is where you need to be.

Cleaner environment

People mess things up, sadly enough. From the black dust kicked up by passing cars through to the scattering of litter and cigarette butts, the more people you have in one area the worse it will look.

This is even worse when large industrial factories enter the picture – suddenly you have smoke filling the sky and pollution filling your streams and rivers. The city is full of grey concrete, pollution, and trash.

Small towns, by contrast, are far cleaner. The pollution-causing industrial manufacturing stays well away, as they need a certain concentration of people and supply chains to work effectively. The scattered population means that there is no central point for those piles of rubbish to materialise. Green fields, forests, and rivers surround the scattered houses. You can happily swim in the local lake, eat from the local fields, breathe deeply from the cold air. You have easy access to home-grown food and almost unspoiled nature starting at your doorway.

What does this mean for you? If you are looking for a clean environment, be it fresh air or wide-open green spaces, then you will need to look to the countryside.

Lower crime

Crime is significantly lower in rural areas. You will rarely have home invasions or burglaries, many people will simply leave their doors unlocked even while away for the weekend. There are also far fewer incidences of street crime, muggings, drunken attacks outside bars or creepy guys spiking drinks. As a general rule, the sense of community tends to shield against the instinct to rob or threaten your neighbours.

This is not to say that there is no crime, because some of the really *weird* cases tend to occur in small towns. Similarly less-populated areas will have a lot of the 'small crimes', things such as speeding, underage drinking, or hunting out of season. More recently the opioid epidemic and other recreational drug use has hit rural towns hard, though these tend to be 'behind the scenes' rather than the out-in-the-open crimes that you see in large cities. If you can accept this trade-off, then smaller towns are truly a paradise to live in.

Cheaper living costs

The general cost of living is far, far lower in rural areas. Most of this is due to your house or apartment – there's generally so much space and so few people that there's very little pressure on house prices. If you're trying to find a mid-sized house for non-outrageous prices, then country living is definitely for you. Fresh food from local farms is also very cheap, letting you feed yourself and your family for very little.

However, you'll need to keep in mind that not everything is cheaper – you'll often find that you pay more for petrol, high-tech equipment, and other things which need to be shipped in from far away. The spread of online shops and marketplaces such as Amazon does help here, provided you are happy with having your purchases sent via the post.

Despite the occasional expensive object, you'll find that *in general* your money will go much further in the countryside. If you are careful to look for low-cost areas, then you can stretch your savings for quite a few years without any stress.

Better life for the children

Smaller towns tend to provide a better environment to raise children. You'll be surrounded by greenery and fresh air, encouraging a healthy and active lifestyle. The lack of crime means you won't stress about your kids riding their bikes on the roads in the evening or walking over to their friend's house for a spontaneous sleepover. You will be enveloped in a close-knit community who will nonetheless expect you to pull your weight, which helps to instil a sense of independence and self-sufficiency in both the parents and their children. Often described as 'small-town values', the experiences and priorities which children are exposed to during those formative years will be essential in creating the adults they will one day become.

Minus points

Nothing is perfect, of course, and there are naturally down-sides to living in the countryside. Most of these have to do with the isolation and lack of people – you'll have limited infrastructure, you'll need to adjust your thinking, the children will eventually want to move away from home, etc. We cover these in more detail below.

Limited facilities and infrastructure

One major disadvantage of rural and small towns is the lack of infrastructure and facilities. With fewer people and less money to throw around, the local government has to prioritise what is most important. Very often this means that the less important, but still useful things tend to fall by the wayside.

Health care is a prime example of this. A major city will have a number of hospitals, well-stocked with experts and with significant experience in treating a wide range of problems. This is rarely the case in small towns – if you are lucky the town will be the home of a regional hospital, if you are unlucky you may have to drive for an hour or two to reach the next one. This also applies to medical specialists and diagnostic labs – it is rare for even a small city to be able to *identify*, let alone treat an 'uncommon' problem.

Nor is this limited to health services, even something as basic as entertainment is also limited in a smaller town. From libraries, bars, theatre or concert halls, the town will simply lack the wide range of entertainment options available in a larger one. Nor are they likely to improve – government funding rarely stretches far enough to sponsor the arts in small towns and instead focuses on large-population areas to get maximum bang for the buck. In other words, you will usually be forced to wander into the next major city to get your cultural fix. Of course, this may not be a problem for you – it depends entirely on what you like to do for entertainment. But you should definitely be *aware* of this before the move.

Infrastructure is also usually less reliable or less efficient in rural areas. The most obvious example here is public transport, there is rarely a reliable bus or train system in place to get you around the region – when one does exist it will usually only run two-three times a day. Because of this families in rural areas are essentially forced to have a car for each adult in the household in order to reach work, the supermarket, home, etc.

Another often-important factor is that of internet access, which can often be erratic or have slower connections that you would expect in the city. If your job involves you being online, or requires reliable access to a connection, then be sure to ask around for the best service provider. Few things are as irritating as the connection going down on a Sunday afternoon when no-one is able to help you out.

This seems somewhat petty and perhaps it is, depending on how important you find your internet to be. But this problem with infrastructure also applies to dealing with *big* problems, major disasters such as flooding, blizzards, or a hurricane. A sudden snowfall will often bring a city to a standstill for a day or so, it can take far longer for a small town to get everything organised. The independence which you need for small-town living also spills over into preparing for the worst.

It requires an adjustment

City life and small town life are different, there is no doubt about it. In general only people who truly accept the lifestyle will be comfortable in a smaller town – those who spend their time in regrets or thinking of their 'lost' city life will tend to give up sooner or later. So if you've lived your entire life in a major urban centre, then you really need to think twice about the change that you're about to bring upon yourself. Some people fall right into the small town feeling and stay forever, some decide that it's just *too* much peace and quiet and decide to leave after a few years.

What does this mean for you? It's important to weigh the advantages and disadvantages with an objective eye. Don't let the romance of small-town life stop you from thinking about what a move will mean to you and your preferred lifestyle. Read through this book, think about what is important for you, personally, and then make a clear-eyed, sensible decision.

Being single is tough

It's very, very hard to be single in a small town. Lots of people will end up married or in committed relationships from a fairly young age, which means there will be fewer unattached ones left. It's a small town, so you'll know most of them (and will probably have dinner with most of them) in a short period of time. If nothing clicks then, well, you'll have to hope that you can find someone for you in the surrounding towns.

So if you're single, or at least not in a long-term relationship, then you should be careful about moving to a rural area. The lack of dating opportunities may not be a problem at the start, but it will eventually start to wear away at you. At the very least try to take up a new hobby where you can meet a large number of people.

Gossip

The stereotype of small towns is that everyone knows everyone, and that everyone knows everyone else's business. And, well, this is true. There is a huge amount of gossip in small towns, particularly centred on new and exciting events – for example, those people who have just moved in from the big city. People will come and talk to you, everyone else will know what you've said and what your conversational partner thought of your comments. Often within a couple of hours.

This also means that you spend a lot of time just chatting or catching up on gossip. Many a weekend morning will be taken up by an unexpected visitor dropping by for coffee and a chat. Quite a lengthy chat too, one which you can't cut short by saying that you really, really need to mow the lawn or do your tax return. These conversations are just another part of small-town living.

We go into this in more detail in a later section (page 58). However it is important to be aware of the prevalence of gossip in smaller towns when deciding if you want to move there.

The children will leave

The countryside and smaller towns are excellent places to raise your kids; they can enjoy fresh air, wide green spaces, and plenty of spots to run around in safety. But eventually they will grow up. The kids become teenagers, then adults, they want to see the world and go to university and get a taste of that city life which they've heard about on TV. They will want things which simply aren't available where you are. Experiences and possibilities which they can only find in a larger metropole.

Which means that, eventually, they'll move away. This is pretty much a given, particularly if you've been raising your kids with a sense of independence and a desire to succeed. It's disappointing, yes, but you will have to accept that one day they'll be moving out and away – and that trying to stop them will only bring you arguments and pain.

So by all means enjoy the small town life with your children, but make sure there is more in your life to keep you happy when that big moving-out day finally comes.

A quick checklist
Making the decision to move into a rural area is a big one, a decision which you really, really want to think about. In addition to the pluses and minuses which we mentioned previously, you might want to run through this quick checklist of questions. If you can answer 'yes' to most of these, then you're ready for the big step.

- Are you ok with being self-reliant, responsible for your own life? Particularly when it comes to things like
- At the same time, are you ok with asking your neighbours for help?
- Can you cope with getting dirty hands in the garden or around the home?
- Are you prepared for the daily activities of country life – tractors, land clearing, pesticide and fertiliser spraying, and harvesting?

- Are you prepared for having a wide range of animals and birds around, (both the wanted ones and the ones which will eat through your vegetable patch in 30 seconds flat)?
- Can you cope with insects and spiders taking up residence everywhere, and are you prepared to wage an unending war against them?
- When you think of your dream life, are you imagining yourself in a rural location?
- If you have kids, have you looked into the school situation?
- Do you have a job lined up in the new location? Are you able to work remotely in your current job? Or are you very confident that you'll find something soon?
- Are you able to work with a spotty internet connection, or have you looked into internet access already?
- Have you got enough money to keep you going for a bit, even if you can't find a job immediately?
- Are you looking for an idyllic property tucked away in the countryside or a louder place with better access to town?
- How far away from the town centre are you willing to live?
- Are you comfortable with driving on badly-lit or narrow roads?
- Do you have a car? Is it reliable? And are you ready for the petrol costs?
- Are you ok with making long drives to reach larger shops or central services?
- Are you able to cook for yourself, rather than living on take-away?

- Have you listed the plus and minus points for your situation, then rationally assessed whether the move makes sense for *you*?

2. Finding a place

So you've look at the pluses and minuses and now you're ready to make the move into a regional area. This is great news! The first big step in the entire process is now done. Unfortunately, it's not the last step.

The next problem which will come up is that of finding the place you actually want to live in. This is a huge decision and one which can have completely different outcomes depending on your personal preferences, the area you are looking at, and the potential budget. This means that it is basically impossible to give advice tailored to your specific situation (because, well, it's your specific situation).

So rather than waffle on for hundreds of pages, we're just going to give some general advice to keep in mind when looking for your dream home in the countryside. The actual process of moving is a separate issue – we've provided a basic checklist for your move in the appendix (page 75), but you'll need to adapt it for your personal situation.

Talk to an agent

Yes, you're going to need a real estate agent to show you around and help you pick out a place. No, you shouldn't try to do it by yourself. If you're worried about finding the right one, then spend a while looking at different ones. Chat to the locals and ask who they would recommend. Look at websites, ask at the town hall for their recommendations. Go visit them in person and look at the windows of the real estate agent – are the listed properties fresh or are they old, faded photos? The second is the sign of either a lazy agent or a terrible set of properties on offer.

When you choose an agent, make sure you give them a list of your requirements and your intended budget. These should have been worked out beforehand, in peace and quiet. They are a reasonable list of what *you need* to have a comfortable life in your new home, so try to stick to it as well as possible. Sometimes agents will show you options slightly outside your intended price range or that don't match your needs. This is fine – some variety is important to help you find the ideal place. But if they *keep* doing it, it's time to move on.

Look at the property

Everyone knows the typical 'location, location, location' cry of the real estate agent. It's true for many reasons, and many of them apply to rural areas. The following section lists just a few of the questions which you should keep in mind when examining a property:

The block

- Is it the right size? Large blocks of land need more work, which means more of your time – and that's mostly coming out of your weekend. Is the block the right size for your planned lifestyle, both in the garden and outside? Do you know the exact boundaries of the property?

- Is the property safe? Have any repairs or renovations been performed by competent professionals, or are you looking at a DIY house-flip?

- How hilly is the area? Sloping hills make for lovely views but difficult gardening, while truly mountainous areas may have you falling off a cliff if you walk the wrong way.

Keep ease of use in mind while planning your future home and garden.

- How good is the soil? If you are planning to grow your own fruit and vegetables, then the quality of the soil will strongly affect your overall yield.

Access to services

- How isolated is it? You may be searching for a property far away from others, but keep in mind that this also puts you far away from important things such as medical services, petrol stations or schools.
- Do you have water access? This is more of a question for rural properties, as most town houses will be on the water network. But you should still know where your water is coming from – will you need to treat it or filter it?
- Do you have access to other important infrastructure? Such as sewage, gas, electricity, internet, phone lines, or mobile reception. If not, how much will it cost you to get this access or to set up replacements?

How is the weather?

- Are you in a flood area? Few things destroy property as much as flooding, and it's often not covered by insurance. Are you *really* sure you want to take the risk?
- What will the year-round weather look like? Do you have snow, bushfires, or sunny summers? Do you need to pay extra for heating or snow-clearing, or include a wider fire-proof zone around the house? Is your driveway accessible under all weather conditions? Do you have long hours of sunshine or are you shaded by surrounding hills?

- How are the roads? Roads in country areas are usually narrow, never lit, and often challenging to travel in bad weather. Are the roads around your new home suitable, and are you personally ok with driving along them on a dark, moonless night?

Legal things

- What sort of local regulations are in place? Will they prevent you from doing things on your property which you have otherwise planned? For example, clearing away trees, building a deck, digging out ground for a pool, etc. Or will you be required to do certain activities (weed control, animal culling) which you would rather avoid?

- Is the land clean? Sadly, a number of places in the countryside have seen chemical spills, mining waste, or over-enthusiastic pesticide use. This can contaminate the land for years to come, so be sure to check for this kind of use in local registries.

- Along these lines, is there mining or other resource extraction happening in the area? Do you have mineral rights which may be sold in the future, or will you come home one evening to find a sink-hole has swallowed up your house?

- Can you sell the property again? If everything goes wrong, do you have an exit strategy? Will the property be tempting for other purchasers, or are you buying in a stagnating area where the block will lie around, unsold, when you need to get out?

The surrounding region

There is more to a house than the block of land, you are also buying a small slice of the local community. This means that any decision needs to take the surrounding region into account as well.

Here are a few factors which you should keep in mind about the local region:

- How are the neighbours? What do the neighbours look like? Will you have death metal blasting until late at night, will you be woken up at the crack of dawn by crowing roosters, does logging happen in the nearby forest? All of this has a major effect on you quality of life.

- How are the local networks? We cover this in later sections (see page 43), but it's important to get into contact with others in the region. Do you know what the local clubs or organisations are, and will they be able to help you out with advice in a pinch?

- Can you identify the local experts? The resident handyman, vet, doctor, butcher, etc. etc. Often these people aren't listed, and they'll rarely have a website. Ask around to find out who you should be talking to.

- Are there jobs around? Assuming that you're not retired, you will need to look at getting a job of some sort in your new home. Are there opportunities around your ideal area? Will you be doing an hour-long commute on top of your nine-to-five? If you work from home, do you have the internet, power and phone access which you'd require? If not, how much will it cost you to get it installed?

The buyer (i.e. you)

Last on the list, but possibly the most important of the factors, is the buyer. In other words, you. What you can afford, manage, and achieve have huge impacts on the property which you can purchase. More often, your physical, financial and mental attributes will provide reasons not to buy a certain property, even though your heart may have fallen in love with the place.

Let's look at a few important questions to ask yourself:

- Can you afford it? This is not just the property, but all the associated taxes and the improvements you want to put in. Everything costs either money or time, so you need to be sure that you can provide enough of both as needed.

- Do you have a financial cushion in case things go wrong or take longer than expected? How much time will you have before things get nasty?

- Especially for those planning on buying a country homestead or living way out of town – are you fit enough? Healthy enough to manage all of the required work? If you are getting on in years (which happens to us all), then it might be worth looking at something easier to deal with.

- Are you *tough* enough? Can you cope with long periods when the power goes down, with clearing fallen branches after a storm, with shovelling snow from our long, long driveway? Can you do all this and then get in your car to drive to work? Are you independent or will you be relying on neighbours for assistance in these matters?

- What does your family think of the idea? Do your kids have a number of different appointments that you'll need to drive them too, or are they happy just to play in the nearby forest? What will they think of the place when they reach their teenage years?

- Do you have pets? Is the local environment suitable for them, or will you have to invest in new haircuts for your dogs, flea collars for your cats, or ways to keep your animals away from the local road?

3. Getting used to your new home

You've picked out the ideal property and you've made the move. Congratulations! The time you spend in the countryside or in a small town will often be some of the best, most relaxing years of your life.

Having said that, starting a new life requires an adjustment, a realisation that the new home is not the same as the old home. An unfortunately large number of people don't manage to make this adjustment, they fail to appreciate the town for *what it is* and instead try to bring the old 'city' way of living into a regional area. These half-hearted newcomers are then suddenly surprised that it doesn't really work, at which point they start complaining and wishing for their old lives back.

How do you avoid this? You need to accept that your new life is *different* to your old one – not worse, but different. There are a few things you can do to help here:

- Enjoy the town for what it is, not for what it isn't
- Remember that small towns have their own histories
- Accept that acceptance will take time

We'll look at these approaches in more detail in the following sections.

Enjoy the town for what it is

One major mistake which many people make is that of comparing everything in their new home to their previous one in 'the city'. By doing this they often focus on the things which they no longer have rather than the new opportunities of the small town. This in turn leads to disappointment, depression, a sense of isolation, and eventually a lingering doubt as to why they moved there in the first place.

How do you avoid this trap? The following sections will provide you with a few hints.

Don't think of it as the sticks

This is possibly one of the most important mental adjustments which you can make. Don't think of the place as 'the sticks', the tiny town where donkeys roam the streets and electricity was only heard of three years ago. Yes, it is a smaller community than the major metropolis you were in before. No, that doesn't mean they are behind the times – the locals will visit nearby cities more often than you expect, they'll watch the same television as you did before, and many of them will be just as tired of their daily email flood as you are.

Information is everywhere these days and work is becoming ever-more decentralised. What was once an isolated town can now be a small hub of off-site programmers, a central trading area, or even the site of a pharmaceutical manufacturing company. That tiny town may be filled with scientists two years later and ten times the size a decade after that. Seems ridiculous? Maybe, but it definitely happens – I've seen it happen myself.

Don't act as though you are superior

The *absolute* worst mistake that you can do when moving to a smaller town is to act as though you are superior to the locals. You should never, ever, (ever!) give any kind of impression that you are smarter or better than your new neighbours. *Nothing* is more likely to make them dislike you.

Keep in mind that this counts for both words and actions, to both people you know well and those you don't. Even an offhand comment to a neighbour can spread throughout the town and soon you will find yourself given a cold shoulder wherever you go.

Don't constantly compare to your past

The second major mistake which many people make is that of comparing everything to their old home. Worse still, they then *complain* about how much better things used to be (and you know exactly the sort of complaints - "the coffee was better", "I used to visit a different museum every weekend", "the grocery store had exotic vegetables", "you call this a craft beer?"). Comparison and complaining will not only make your life more miserable, but will give people the impression that you want your new home to be just like your old home. At this point they will wonder why you are here at all, assume you will leave soon anyway, and not put in the effort to get to know you.

This is, unsurprisingly, the quickest route to feeling isolated in the community.

You may find that the locals complain about these sort of things. Quite often, in fact. But, unfortunately, you will still have to hold your tongue. It takes many years of living in a small town before people will accept your right to complain about it.

So how do you avoid this problem? Try to avoid 'replicating' your previous activities or environment in the new town. This is both doomed to failure (a small town isn't a big city, no matter how much you try) and inevitably depressing (as you spend too much time focused on your past). The new place *is different*, so embrace that and accept it for what it is – look forward to the new opportunity, not back to the old.

This same acceptance of the 'new' approach is also important when trying to change your new community. Think of newcomers who join the local political system, school boards, even the local cake and knotting clubs. Trying to persuade everyone to do things because 'that's how it's done in the city' is a sure-fire way to have your ideas ignored, regardless of how good they are. A good rule of thumb is to always work *within the existing system*. In other words, take the new system as it is, don't compare it to the old one.

Find your own joy

Regional communities lack many of the entertainment options which you may have been used to in the larger city. But this doesn't mean there is nothing to do. Instead, it is *up to you* to find your own entertainment, your own sources of joy. Entertainment, like many situations in regional areas, is something which calls for ingenuity and self-reliance from the inhabitants.

So where do you find your inner sense of happiness? There are many sources, be it the quiet of the street as you go for a morning jog, the fresh breeze which flows through the town as you drink a leisurely coffee, the sun setting over green farmland as you and your friends enjoy a glass of beer. There will be many ways in which you can enjoy your new life rather than regretting the enjoyment you used to have.

There are less people in the countryside, this is true, so you'll need to find things you love to do – with or without people by your side. Many of these will work with the more relaxed atmosphere – read a book, enjoy a lazy Sunday afternoon, go fishing in a local lake. We've collected a list of possible hobbies you might want to look into in a later chapter (page 67).

Still stuck for ideas? Feel free to ask people for suggestions or tips, they'll often be happy to share their knowledge with people who are *genuinely* interested. Note the 'genuinely', because no-one wants to deal with that guy who asks "man, it's so dull, what can you do for fun around here?" Don't be that guy.

Slow down

Life is more relaxed and bit slower in small towns – this is often the reason why people move out there in the first place. You'll need to accept and embrace this if you want to avoid getting frustrated in your daily routine.

So take your time, stop to chat with people, wave to others when driving past, honk to say hello, take a relaxed attitude to the small annoyances of life. Remember that being pushy or hurried will rarely get you to your goal in time. And doing this will cause others in town to respect you less – and respect is extremely important in a small town.

Be a tourist

Tourism is fun – it's a great way to see new places and experience new things. But you don't need to travel halfway around the world to be a tourist, it's entirely possible to be a tourist in your own region. Start out by checking the sights listed in local travel guides, or in the town hall visitors' guides. These are the 'big' things that your area is known for, things which your friends and visitors will have heard about in one way or another. Thus you should really know what they are and how they look, if for no other reason than to answer questions from your friends.

But there are always more things to see, those which aren't listed in the local guidebook. These are more difficult to find, but as you get to know the locals, they'll be more willing to share the less-well-known sites. This is particularly the case if you've already shown interest in seeing what the area has to offer.

Get comfortable with driving

Public transport in regional areas is inevitably underfunded and sporadic. You might be able to catch a bus, but it certainly won't be happening all that often. This means you need to be comfortable with driving yourself around town and in the countryside. You will also need a car for each adult in the household – particularly if you are working in separate locations or if there are kids that need to be picked up from school.

Country traffic is lighter than city peak hour, of course. But it comes with its own set of challenges, whether it's dark and winding streets, bridges washing away in bad storms, getting caught behind a tractor on a narrow road, or simply slow-moving herds of cows refusing to get off the road. You'll need to adjust to this if you want to make the countryside your new home.

And, of course, what if you aren't a fan of driving *at all*? Then, well… you will have to learn. Otherwise you will never really feel comfortable in your new home.

Remember that small towns have their own histories

One common mistake which new arrivals make is to assume that nothing really happens in a small town. They look around, see a few shops or a quiet streets, and then decide that because nothing is going on *right now* that nothing has really happened *at any time previously*.

This is far from the truth, every town is founded for a reason and most of them will have histories dating back decades and centuries. It may have started as a farming village from the Middle Ages, a boom town from the gold-rush era, even a chance crossing of two roads which (naturally) required a pub, around which the settlement grew. There is a wealth of history behind even the smallest two-horse town, a history which has been around well before you were born and will be there well after you die. Try not to misjudge it.

This also applies to the *people* in the town – history is built on people, after all. Small towns will be full of people who have known each other since childhood, they were friends or enemies in school, they hung out together as teenagers, they worked together in fields or mines or big-box supermarkets. Any friendships and grudges will be far more intense than you would see in a larger city. There are fewer people, they interact with each other more often, there are no chances for those emotions to fade. You will find people hating one another for a slight argument twenty years ago, or sometimes even for slight arguments their great-grandparents had. It may seem silly, yes, but you will need to get used to it. No-one wants to hear the new people telling them that their long-held grudges are built on petty problems, no-one wants to feel judged by those who do not fully understand their long history.

This is even more apparent when politics enter the picture. Political power in small towns is often built on generations of respectable jobs, underhand dealings, arguments over local issues, and wealth. Don't judge an entire town's politics on the basis of a single website, but be aware that the number of 'sides' in politics will be far more limited than you are normally used to. The divisions between the groups will also be more obvious, again based on a long history of believing different things.

So what should you do? Can you avoid being wrapped up in the politics and feuding of the town? In general you should take the common-sense approach to being polite. Try to simply accept that the people in your new town will believe some things that you disagree with or that you don't understand. Does this affect you? No? Then just let it be. Ignore the issue and go about your life. Be generous and tolerant with everyone you meet, and soon enough the town will respect you for being a good person. If their beliefs do affect you, then by all means make this clear. Just do it in a clear and polite way, rather than descending into a shouting match or vicious argument. Manners are important, after all.

Accept that acceptance takes time

When you arrive in town you'll probably be looking forward to making new friends, part of the process of settling into your new home and town. Unfortunately you'll need to dial back on your enthusiasm and accept that things may take a bit longer than you expect – friendship is a slow process in the countryside.

This is particularly the case if you're trying to become 'just' another one of the locals. The smaller the town, the more strict the definition of who is a local and who just moved there. Often even people who have been in town for decades are still considered the 'new guys'.

So how do you get yourself started on the road to acceptance? Be patient and accept that it will take a while before you're really into the local community. Take advantage of social offers when they occur (the spontaneous invitation to dinner or lunch), but don't force people to constantly interact with you. Pushing yourself onto others will go against the small-town pace, making you look hurried, needy, and somehow weird. You'll find that projecting an image of friendly authenticity will get you a long way in the community.

People talk, of course, which means that after a few weeks you'll be meeting people who already know who you are and where you live. That's perfectly fine, see it as an opportunity to springboard the conversation into more important topics. Ask the locals for advice, on good doctors, where to buy specific things, where you can get wood for the fireplace and how parcel deliveries work. Nothing pulls you into a local community than asking the opinions of a few well-connected people and having them take you under their wings.

4. Making friends

There's nothing worse than sitting at home, alone, wishing that you could go talk to someone but not knowing anyone to talk to. If you want to enjoy your new life in a country area then you're going to need to make some new friends.

Maybe you're a natural socialiser, in which case this isn't really a problem. But others of us are a bit less certain and a bit more worried about what we should do. If you're in the second group, then this section will give you a few hints and tips which you can follow.

More specifically, we'll cover:

- The importance of giving a good first impression
- Quick tricks to become more accepted
- The importance of joining a social club

We also have dedicated chapters for those who are worried about gossip (page 58) or dealing with a sense of boredom or loneliness (page 65).

First impressions count

Possibly the most useful advice anyone can give to newcomers in a small town – be friendly. It's not like the big city where you are a single face in a sea of humanity. In a small town, people will notice you. They'll want to say hi, they'll remember that you walked right past them with a blank look on your face. You will need to get used to the way people want to stand and talk. Even if you're not much of a small-talker, you should try to spend a few minutes catching up.

So what does this mean specifically?

Say hello

Say hi to people. In general everyone will be friendly, even on bad days, so you'll be able to have a quick chat with almost anyone you meet. Friends, neighbours, folks down at the store, you name it, they'll be happy to talk.

The flip-side of this is that saying 'how are you' is no longer just a polite phrase to throw into a conversation before heading your own way. It's an actual question, one which the conversation partner will be expected to answer. You'll probably end up in a five-minute chat after this 'quick' question, so try to avoid it if you're in a rush. Once you've said it, however, then stay for the entire talk! Running away in the middle of a 'how are you' conversation will give you a stuck-up or uncaring reputation.

This doesn't mean that you always have to talk, of course. But you should at least try to *acknowledge* people you meet – smile, wave, nod, do the two-fingers-raised-from-the-steering-wheel-wave, say hi. It's a simple thing but it does wonders for your relationships with the neighbours.

While you're at it, find out what your local greeting is – do people say hi, hello, howdy, g'day, etc.? Try to use that phrase with others, it's a simple way to blend into the community and reduce your 'outsider' impression.

Respect others

The basic rule in small towns and large cities is the same – don't be an idiot. People in towns are generally easy going and will be nice to you if you are nice to them. This makes the path to acceptance pretty easy to follow – be polite and respectful in your dealings with everyone. Above all avoid thinking that as a 'city transplant' you are better than your neighbours (better educated, smarter, more qualified, etc.). This is the fastest possible way to turn everyone against you.

Many people move to more regional areas because they want to have a bit more freedom – freedom from neighbours, pollution, noise, etc. They may not appreciate you taking up their time, particularly if they've grown used to having a lot of free time for themselves. You should respect this need, don't overwhelm them with your personality at the start.

This means that the best approach when moving into a new place is simply to arrive quietly, don't decorate like a madman, and go about your business. Mow your lawn, shop at the local store, smile. You'll find that the neighbours will start approaching you, wanting to find out who you are and what you're up to – this is the start of the process of building friends.

Becoming more than 'the newcomer'

We covered the basics above, but actually *becoming* part of the community is a lot more challenging than simply smiling at everyone you meet. If you've just moved to a small town or rural area then it can take years to truly feel like you belong, just because the few locals who live there have generations-worth of history. To help you, we've collected a couple of handy hints to become more than just 'the new guy' or 'the new girl'.

Be patient

One of the challenging parts of moving to a smaller community is making *real* friends and connections. Small towns have routines, the people who live there already have friends, favourite activities, hobbies which they spend their time doing. This means that they don't have spare time for new things or new people, (i.e. those who have just moved in from the city and are looking to get to know everyone).

So what does this mean? It means that you need to have a bit of patience. You can't go barging into people's lives, trying to make them into your friend. Instead, you'll have to take the slower approach. This can be maddeningly slow at times – sometimes it will feel that it takes five years before you're invited to private celebrations and ten before they think of you as being just like regular folks. But it will happen, and you will make some truly wonderful friendships within the community.

Be polite

Politeness is a pretty big topic, and one which is basically beyond our ability to cover in a book of this size. However here are a couple of basic things which tend to be seen as more important in the countryside than in the city.

- Wave to or acknowledge people when you're passing by (this also includes when you're in the car, though you can get away with a subtle lift of two fingers from the steering wheel).
- Stop to talk to people when you see them at the store or in the street. This applies even more so when you see your neighbours.
- Actually *listen* to what people are saying – ask questions and follow-up on their comments
- If you did something wrong, or you're imposing on another, then at least say 'sorry'
- Keep up with those 'old fashioned' manners – hold the door open for others, thank people for their help, show respect to the elderly, etc.

- Share with your neighbours. If you're going to be baking, make a bit extra and drop by your neighbour's house for a visit. If you are setting up the barbeque, offer them a few beers. Sharing builds relationships, particularly in rural areas.

- If someone lends you something, especially if it's a container of some sort, then never return that container empty – fill it with some chocolates, a bottle of wine, even just a heap of apples.

Remember that not everyone wants to chat

Small towns are full of interesting characters, many of whom have ended up there because they want to get away from the hustle and bustle of city life. This often includes getting away from the people – residents have traded the crowded streets of the city for the open air and solitude of the countryside. Their love of solitude means you'll rarely run into them at parties or get-togethers, they'd rather be off in the woods or working one of the fields.

But solitary types often make great friends, once you've gotten past their protective shell. You'll meet them through random shared hobbies or through extended friends of friends, and once the initial awkward period is over you'll find that – although they don't say much – what they *do* say is worth listening to.

The key is to remember that not everyone *wants* to chat and not everyone *needs* to chat. People who always hang around wanting to talk will give off a needy impression, something which will drive away the typically self-reliant types who end up in small towns. Instead, you should try to cultivate a slightly mysterious or aloof nature, don't share all of your secrets at once and don't instantly try to make people your best buddies. Be casual, and things will work out.

Conversation topics

Conversation can be a bit tricky sometimes, especially when you're in a very small town where opinions are homogenous and alternatives aren't really accepted. A good rule of thumb is to avoid talking about religion and politics for a while. By all means go for it when you've been around for longer and you're more integrated into the community. By this point you should know which topics are acceptable for discussion. Until then, stay with the safe ones – sports, weather, and complaints about tourists.

The other topic which will always come up is a simple one – how do you fit into the town? Most people will want to know the answer to three basic questions: Where do you come from? Why did you choose to move here? Do you have relatives or friends here already? This set of questions will *always* come up when talking to people in town. It can get repetitive, yes, but you can at least rehearse a couple of simple answers to get the conversation flowing more smoothly. 'Why you came here' is also a great topic as it allows you to talk for ages about the nicest parts of living in your town – and locals always like to hear about how nice their area is, which makes this a safe and entertaining topic.

Hang out at the local

Every town has a local pub, the bar where everyone goes, where the bartender knows your name and what you want to drink and where there's a 'hall of fame' showing the guy who won the latest burger-eating competition. You know the type. It's usually in the centre, in really small towns it will be at the main intersection (just across from the town hall) and it's often one of the oldest buildings around. This is where you want to be.

Become a regular at the local tavern. Make sure you follow the dress code, if there is one, and order something which is on tap.

Be friendly and polite, and don't forget to tip. There aren't many activities which will get you involved in the local community like hanging out at the pub.

Have a baby

If you really want to be welcomed with open arms, then carry a baby around with you. This is obviously not helpful for everyone (though perhaps you can borrow a baby for a day), but if you do have a baby then you will quickly find yourself wrapped up in the arms of the community. Many people who live in small towns do so for their children, almost all will be happy to see a smiling (if exhausted) young family.

Give back to the town – and make some friends on the way

There are many different community groups which pop up in small towns, often in numbers which are completely out of proportion to the population. They will run regular events, host fundraising and charity do's, and generally serve as a hub for socialising. Joining a community group is an excellent way to get yourself into the community, you'll meet new people with similar interests in a relaxed environment. And naturally, there is always a lot to do and never enough people to do it – thus new faces are always welcome.

How do you find these groups? Very few of them will have a website or internet presence, so you can skip your plan of 'just looking online'. Instead you will need the old-fashioned method of 'asking around'. Ask your neighbours, ask at the town hall, ask at the store, you can even ask the community leaders. Everyone will know someone who can direct you further. For those who don't really like the idea of talking to people, check for bulletin boards at local gathering places – the library, the church, the community centre, even the central sports club. There'll be flyers for all sorts of groups, just have a look and decide what interests you.

One thing should always be kept in mind, whichever group you end up attending. New faces are always welcome, but you should be careful to come in with an open mind and a willingness to do things the way they are *currently* done. Don't try to take over everything yourself, don't try to change the systems to something which is 'clearly' better. This will just cause resentment and anger in your co-volunteers, removing any of the good-will which you may have built up by attending in the first place. Be patient and humble!

Sounds interesting? There are a number of different community groups which you may want to join.

Church
The life of many small towns revolves around the church. There are many different religions, of course, and you'll find that any particular town has a number of different ones on offer. If you are religious, then this is a perfect place to start – turn up, say hi, and before you know it you will be slotting into a well-oiled social machine. This also applies even if you don't attend church all that often. You may find that there is more pressure to come each week but in general people will simply be glad to know that you are there on occasion.

The downside of this is that *not* attending church does sometimes seem a bit odd to your neighbours, particularly in highly religious areas. A good compromise in these cases is to visit church 'events', get-togethers outside of regular services such as dinners, cake-sales or barbeques. These are not as explicitly religious as a church service would be, yet still let you meet and chat with your neighbours in a relaxed setting. You'll still get the occasional question as to when you'll attend a service, but this is just a price you pay for the delicious food.

Social volunteers

Although churches are often the largest organised groups in any town, there will still be a number of other groups if you would rather do your social volunteering in a non-religious way. These can include the Rotary Club or the Lions Club for social work, Red cross or volunteer firefighters for those who want to help in emergencies, even the local aged-care centre will need volunteers to help get their residents to doctor's appointments and the like. There is generally no lack of things which you could do to help the community, the trick is to figure out which of these is right for you. Ask around, check the local noticeboards, visit once or twice to see if the members match your needs. You'll always be welcome.

Preservation groups and other societies

Preservation societies are another group which often pops up in regional areas. They have a number of different names, stereotypically something along the lines of "Society for Preservation of X", where X is a local landmark or natural feature. If you have an environmental or cultural bent, then these will bring you in touch with like-minded people. Other clubs with similar goals include library groups (e.g. "Friends of the library") for those who are interested in reading and literature. Alternatively, if you're interested in local history, historical societies are a great place to make contacts and discuss how the place has grown over the years.

Regardless of their specific aims, each of these clubs will focus on raising money for their own particular cause. This means your volunteer work will inevitably include some sort of fundraising, very often involving cooking food or selling cakes. This is *certainly* not the worst thing to do with your time, particularly as you get to eat the left-overs.

One thing you will need to keep in mind is that most members of such societies are usually fairly old, tending towards retirement age. If this matches your age, then this is naturally a perfect way to meet new friends. However these societies can be great fun even if you are younger – the other members will love the fact that the 'next generation' is getting involved in their local issues and will happily introduce you to their children and grandchildren. This is an excellent way to grow your network across many levels of society.

Local traditions

Every community has traditions, from the smallest town to the largest city. Traditions lead to celebrations, because everyone likes an excuse for a party, and celebrations need to be organised in some way or another. Which is, naturally enough, a good point for someone new in town to step in. Whether it's decorating floats for the town parade, running a stall or cleaning up piles of trash after everything is done, volunteers are always needed to help keep the tradition alive for the community. If you find fulfilment in seeing others celebrate and want to meet like-minded folks, then this can be a great way to get 'into' the local feeling.

Local politics

Local politics is also a great way for new people to get involved with the community. For those who are interested in gaining status or getting in touch with the elite, joining the political circle offers a simple way to start this process.

Having said this, if you're going to move into local politics, then start *small!* It's a tight-knit group which is very difficult to break into, and you'll be starting with a disadvantage as an outsider. Avoid going for the 'medium-importance' roles such as the select board, school board or town clerk until you get a bit of experience and make a few more contacts (avoid running for Mayor in your first year as well!). Smaller assistant-level roles get you involved without threatening anyone's power base.

Similarly there are a number of committees which hold considerable power in their own area, but which tend to be ignored by the wider population. Think of the local business committee or the town planning committee. These tend to be niche areas filled with successful businesspeople and thus provide excellent opportunities for networking.

As with the other organisations, don't rush to join every civic group you see. This always gives an impression that the new guy is here to 'shake things up', making everyone immediately defensive. This is not to say that you can't change things – to be honest most committees you join will be old-fashioned and fond of doing things because "that's how we've always done it". A bit of fresh air would definitely do them good. But you have to be *subtle* in how you bring about change – don't force it, but encourage it.

Start your own

There are many different clubs in small towns, but there won't be everything. If you have some sort of skill or interest which you're passionate about, then why not start your own group? It may be a book club, chess group, sewing club, even a sports team – the important thing is that it gives everyone (including yourself) a new way to meet others with similar interests.

Starting your own club can be a bit daunting and you may want to wait until you're more comfortable in the community (in particular knowing how everything is done there). But it's a great way to contribute back to the town – and you'll find that even the most obscure hobbies will have one or two interested people who want to join.

5. Being part of the local community

Small towns live and die on the strength of their communities. There are small towns in which everyone knows one another, pulling together in good times and in bad. These towns are a joy to live in and will fulfil every one of the stereotypes which you've seen in the movies. Then there are towns where people come home to sleep, then leave again. Where the main street shops long since closed up due to competition from big-box stores, and where you never see enough people to learn their names.

This may seem a bit exaggerated (and perhaps it is), but the feeling of community is *strongly* dependent on the actions of everyone who lives there. This includes you. Because you're now a resident of the community as well.

So how do you help improve the community feeling? There are a few points which you should keep in mind.

- Buy from local stores wherever possible
- Learn to trust your neighbours
- Keep up-to-date on local issues
- Try to join a social club (we covered this in the previous section).

We cover the first three of these points in a bit more detail in the following sections.

Buy local

In general you should try to buy local whenever you can. Your local stores are run by residents, they provide jobs to your direct community. This makes them a direct source of employment for a large portion of your neighbours, the money which they earn is inevitably spent in other local stores. This is in stark contrast to the big box stores, (think of Walmart as the typical example here) which sell many different things and provide a number of jobs in a single, isolated location, and where the majority of profits flow to out-of-town owners.

Why is this important? A town will generally have a number of smaller stores clustered along a main street or in a shopping district. These clusters attract many more customers than those stores would if they were scattered across a larger distance – you might not bother to drive to one store on a Saturday, but you would if you could get all the shopping done and buy lunch at the same time. By shopping local you support all of these people at once – even if you don't buy something at each store, the presence of many people makes it a more tempting place to be for others.

Big box stores, by contrast, are normally located somewhere out of town. The cheaper prices tend to draw people to that isolated location, which in turn thins out the crowd in the town centre. Less people, less income for the local stores, which means stores begin to close. Closing stores mean fewer visitors to the remainder, making a vicious spiral until the main street is a row of closed and shuttered windows. Which in turn ruins any sense of community which may have been present.

Seems slightly overstated? Sadly no, this exact change has happened to many small towns across the US and indeed throughout the world. Try your hardest to keep your money within the local community by doing as much business as possible with local merchants – be they grocers, banks, gas stations, or plumbers.

Trust others

Regional areas emphasise strong connections between the residents – you will know more people and they will know you. These connections take away a lot of the anonymous 'face in the crowd' feeling which you have in the city. Thus when your neighbours have problems, you'll know about it. And you'll care about them.

This applies in both directions, naturally, and so a small town will have an intricate web of people who are interested in each other's success or survival. Whenever an emergency occurs – flooding, heavy snowfalls, etc., you'll have people looking out for one another, sharing food, giving lifts to the elderly or sick. But it's also a factor in 'smaller', more personal emergencies – if you are having trouble with income, the local church will help organise food to tide you over.

Building trust is vital to becoming part of the community, both the trust you have in the community and the trust they have in you. It comes in two parts, the practical side (people rely on you as a competent and dependable person) and the emotional side (people know that you'll treat them well and feel they can confide in you). Your feelings about the community will come with time, but it is certainly possible to help the neighbours come to trust you. How? Just follow a set of simple principles:

- Tell the truth
- If you don't know something, then say so
- If you're wrong, admit it, and take responsibility
- If you say that you will do something, do it
- If you *should* do something, do it
- Give people trust to receive it in return

- Include other people in your thinking and planning
- Let other people talk, and actually listen to them

Crime

Small towns generally have lower crime rates than larger cities. The population is smaller, more people know one another, and so the number of 'anonymous' crimes such as burglary tend to be far lower. This means you can drop a lot of the paranoia which you'd normally have in the city regarding crime prevention. Small towns usually have so little crime that people routinely forget to lock their houses. This is not to say that you should do the same (crime is everywhere, after all), but you can probably skip installing motion-activated lights or other 'obvious' security features. Particularly those which are sensitive enough to detect people walking their dogs along the street – this is a sure-fire way to irritate your neighbours.

Stay up-to-date

The best way to keep up to date is simply to read the local newspaper. Rural towns and stores often have very little in the way of a web presence, which means that information still predominantly comes via gossip or the, for more 'official' news, the newspaper.

A local paper acts as a great source of information for everything which is going on, often containing facts which you would otherwise not pick up. The most useful of these are often related to politics (decisions from the town hall meeting, budget proposals, etc.), businesses (new stores opening up or others closing down) and land-use related topics (the local river is being dammed, a paddock will be turned into a nature reserve). All of these have the chance to affect you, which means that it's important to keep informed.

Even if you aren't particularly interested in the inevitable soft news (e.g. "Mrs X, who has been growing geraniums for 50 years, says…") then you should still read the paper to find out what is going on in the town. The paper will have information on upcoming events, be they fundraising dinners, balls and parties, talent shows, etc. If you aren't involved in a community group such as a local church, this is one of the few ways to get a complete overview of the social life of the town.

Be aware of local issues

There are many issues which will be particularly important to your local region, even if they do not make much of a wave in the wider state. It's important for you to keep up to date on these issues as well, not only because it comes up in every conversation but because they will often be important to *you* as well.

So how do you do this and what do you need to keep in mind?

Local politics

Local politics is basically the lowest level of public administration, the one which deals with issues surrounding the local region (and no more). Local government has no say in declaring war, but they can certainly tell you not to build that house. This makes them very important within a regional area, as many of the local issues described in this section are reliant on decisions made by the local government.

One unfortunate constant in almost every small town is that political power tends to *cluster*. You'll find that a small group of people, heavily connected by family or marriage connections, will have the majority of the political appointments and positions. They will have close relationships with the 'important' people in the area – the major business or farm owners, the wealthy residents, etc. And you will find that political decisions, when not major issues for the majority of residents, will somehow tend to benefit that close-knit group.

You may believe that this isn't the best sign of a healthy democracy and, well, you would be right. Unfortunately, however, this is just the way things go. Changing local politics, particularly as a newly-arrived resident, is an exercise in frustration and futility. You may find it easier simply to accept the current state of affairs and just go about your life.

Land rights

The ways in which you can use your land is bound up with the permission given by your local government. Local laws control many different factors about your land – including what you can do, how long you can do it for, and what you have to pay for the privilege.

As a rule of thumb people in regional areas will be more interested in land right issues than those in the cities. This is fair enough, as there is a lot *more land* in the countryside and the use of that land is often how residents make their income. This covers a number of different topics, such as the following:

- Zoning regulations – what use is the land assigned to, and what use could be allowed if the zones were reassigned
- Land tax – the amount of money which owners need to pay local government in order to hold their property
- House improvements – whether council approval is needed in order to build extensions to your house, cut down trees, build an outdoor fire-pit, etc.

- Access rights – whether people on one block have automatic right of way to cross another. This is often set up informally but will occasionally go down to the town hall for decisions.

- Water rights – access to community water for drinking or for irrigation (particularly important for farmers), as well as how that access is provided (via wells, pipes from a central location, etc.). This also includes sewage disposal and the digging of new wells.

- General property rights – the assorted things which you can and cannot do on your property, ranging from burning rubbish through to raising cattle.

- The interaction between residential and agricultural zones – farmers have different priorities to home-dwellers, which can lead to large arguments over lighting, chemical use, erosion, weeds, etc. You name it, it will have come up somewhere.

Although many of these topics may not be important to you *personally*, you can be assured that they are of vital importance to some of your neighbours. Be ready to hear hours' worth of discussion at your next town-hall meeting if a major change to one of these comes up.

Hunting and gun rights

The right to own a gun or go hunting is often a very politically-charged one, particularly in places such as the USA. You will find that opinions on both will be very different between your old and your new home. Part of this comes down to the differing viewpoints of city and country residents. For those in the city a gun is something which they don't need in their daily life, this makes it a foreign object which is rarely seen and thus only held by criminals. In the countryside, a gun is a tool, something which almost every family has and which is *respected* but not *feared*. This different in viewpoint is the source of many disagreements about gun control and the like. Regardless of your opinion, it is important to see where the other person is coming from and to understand why they hold their opinion.

At the same time, hunting is much more common in rural areas, if only for the simple reason that there is more to hunt (deer taste better than rats, after all). This doesn't normally affect new arrivals, though you will definitely have access to more fresh game meat than you would in the city. However you should definitely be ready for the crackling of gunshots which mark the start of the hunting season, and be prepared to wear bright orange vests if you go tramping through the woods around that time. No, it's not the most flattering of colours, but it does make it *very* obvious that you aren't a deer in the bushes. Accidents happen, so stay on the safe side.

Religion

This sense of religious feeling and community is usually far stronger in smaller towns that it would be in larger cities. Keep in mind that 'church issues' will end up affecting community opinion in ways which you may not expect. This also spills over into general cultural values and the actions which people will expect from you. A simple example comes from the experience of moving to a small town with a strong evangelical trend – one which heavily discourages working on Sundays. If you do find yourself working on a Sunday, you'll probably stand out for your 'lack of respect', a factor which can affect your efforts at fitting in for years to come.

So how do you avoid putting your foot in your mouth? Try not to be outspokenly anti-religion if possible, and definitely avoid insulting others for their belief. In general, even if you don't share the beliefs of your new community, you should at least respect them.

Fundraising

Just the same as in the city, there's never enough money to get everything done. Buildings need to be restored, paths need to be repaired, the church wants to organise clothes for the local poor, and everyone worries about children at Christmas. Local government taxes won't come anywhere near solving these problems, and so the community will need to step up themselves in order to fix things.

In practice this means large numbers of fundraising drives, whether its people knocking on your door or little old ladies selling cakes down by the church on Sunday. This rarely raises a large amount of money, but it is enough to do some good in the region and helps to instil the feeling that the community, as a whole, is *doing something*. Those who don't participate in fundraising drives, who ignore or brush off this part of the local society, are therefore seen as not really being part of the community. In other words, exactly the image you want to avoid as a newcomer.

So what should you do? Easy – you should support the charitable efforts of your neighbours, particularly when it doesn't really cost you much. The classical example is when the local kids set up a lemonade stand or sell chocolate bars, etc. Yes, you could get it for cheaper somewhere else. No, the lemonade probably won't be very good. Yes, you should still buy it anyway. Just humour them, it's the polite and neighbourly thing to do.

6. Dealing with gossip

The stereotype of small towns is that they are hotbeds of gossip, with information flashing from one side of the town to another at faster than the speed of light. And to be honest, this is entirely true. Gossip is *everywhere* in a small town, and *everyone* will try to find out what the others are doing.

Does this seem exaggerated? Not at all! From personal experience I can describe old women with binoculars on the kitchen bench to keep track of the neighbours, neighbours 'dropping by' when they see we have a new visitor or large package, even phone calls to tell me that my daughter has bought new shoes on the way home from school. Because, dear Lord, they were blue!

Gossip ends up as a type of currency, one which is sometimes more valuable than cash. Everyone will want to know the latest information and they'll be willing to trade whatever they know for something new. What does this mean? Three things really:

- You need to be very careful in your interactions with others
- You don't really have any privacy, unless you truly work for it
- You need to watch out for the sin of over-interpretation

Let's look at these in a bit more detail in the following sections.

Be careful with your interactions

The first thing you need to keep in mind is that your interactions with others will *inevitably* be judged or spoken about in some way. Not all of them, naturally, even the dullest of small towns has other things to talk about, but enough that others will generally know what you've been doing and saying.

This makes it important for you to be honest and open in your dealings. Don't try to play one group off against another, don't be friendly to peoples' faces and then call them the nastiest things in the world behind their backs. You should avoid treating people differently based on who you think is watching. This *will* get noticed, particularly in a small town, and you'll earn an untrustworthy reputation before you know it.

It also helps to avoid becoming part of the local gossip network. Feel free to listen to everything, but don't spread the news further. This helps you to avoid getting caught up in the local drama and helps avoid making the mistake of gossiping to the wrong person. This is particularly dangerous in regional areas because there are a number of background networks connecting people by birth, marriage, jobs, or shared hobbies – no matter who you meet, they will probably be connected to the next person you run into. As a newcomer you may not notice these networks, but rest assured that they are there. And you'll inevitably discover their existence when you say something nasty to one person about some third party, only to discover that your conversation partner is actually their hairdressers' sisters' babysitter. And then that's it, you've made an enemy.

Sounds a bit ridiculous? Yes, but it happens all the time. Be the silent and stone-faced listener who never spreads gossip beyond their closest circle of friends. This is the best way to gain respect in any small community.

One extra note to this topic – be *particularly* careful with your interactions with the police. Few people hold a grudge like the local policeman, and few people can make your life in town as much of a misery if they don't like you. Don't speed in town, slow down in the school zone, keep your registration up to date – all of these things are usually ignored in the city but will be jumped on by officers with more time on their hands. And when that happens you'll have started on a slow road to being 'the new guy who's a criminal'. Try to avoid this.

You have no privacy

The other side of gossip is that, naturally enough, everyone knows everyone else's business. Any sort of secret which people do have will somehow, mysteriously, manage to make its way out into the general knowledge that the town has. Nothing specific, naturally, but more in the sense of I-heard-from-X-who-heard-from-Y-that… Do one stupid act and before you know it the entire town will have heard about it.

So what does this mean for you?

People are nosey

The residents in small towns tend to pay a lot more attention to each other, simply because there are so few people compared to large, anonymous cities. Pretty much everything about you, whether it be your clothes, your lifestyle, your weekly purchases, or your postal deliveries will get noticed in some way or another. If it's outside the 'normal' range then you can also expect people to start talking about it. Word will get around quite quickly too – I've had comments from random shopkeepers asking about the latest postcard which I'd received, which itself was delivered by a completely unrelated person.

This is particularly the case if you've had or are about to have a big lifestyle change. Moved to a new job? People will be congratulating you, though they may not quite understand what you do. Expecting a baby? Everyone will congratulate you, often somehow knowing the due date, and you'll find little cards and gifts popping up at random times as it gets closer.

This nosey attitude is common enough that people who don't play into it will be seen as somehow odd. If you regularly keep your curtains drawn, or avoid chatting to your neighbour when getting out of the car, then people will think you're weird. Even worse, they'll think you're "up to something" and so will try *even harder* to figure out what it is. Speaking as someone who has had neighbours keep binoculars to 'keep an eye on things', this can only get more and more irritating.

However, it doesn't always have to be annoying. It often helps to simply consider it part of the environment, like the fresh air or rolling farmland, and then be amused by the utterly unexpected connections which you'll see in the gossip network. Even more usefully, you can use this to your advantage. There will be a number of neighbours 'just stopping by' in the first couple of weeks after you've moved in – though most are at least polite enough to wait a few days until you're settled. They'll say hi, want to get to know you, ask where you're from, etc. This is actually a golden opportunity to get your better side out into the community. So take a bit of time, chat, be friendly, have a cup of coffee or tea together. The first contacts you make will inevitably spread their impressions of you throughout the town, so make it a good one!

Get reliable friends

As we've mentioned, secrets tend to get out quickly and so your best bet is to avoid having secrets to hide. This is, well, pretty difficult. So the better, more realistic option is to make sure that you have friends that you can trust. People who you can tell things to without worrying that they'll run off and spread the information within an hour or two.

Difficult to do? Yes, it is. You'll need to keep an eye on people and listen out for the signs that they are reliable or incurable gossips. Try to keep things to yourself until you've figured out who is who. And once you have found reliable friends, hold onto them with all your might.

Decide if you want to be openly different or not

All of this advice seems sensible enough, but sometimes you just want to do something which isn't part of the 'sanctioned' activities that everyone expects you to do. Whether it's following your pagan religion, building up your collection of 90s action figures, enjoying a chai latte or living your dominatrix lifestyle, it is sometimes important *not* to fit in with the standards – particularly when it makes up an important part of your personality.

If this is the case then you have two basic options. One is to simply go about your business as you want to – build a stone circle, buy a ninja turtle, make the drink, set up the dungeon. In this situation you are *guaranteed* to become an item of discussion for the town, even attempting to keep a low profile will eventually be found out. The question is more *whether you care*. All gossip blows over eventually, the next bit of news will come along or the next teenage pregnancy will occur and people will stop discussing your personal life. But they will definitely remember it, and this knowledge will probably affect how they interact with you. In particular, if your 'difference' involves something that offends conservative opinions then you are likely to have difficulty in a small towns.

The other option is to hide this part of yourself. This is generally not a good thing, you'll feel stifled and somehow trapped, but it may be the best way to avoid the opinions of others. If this is the case then you should make sure to schedule regular trips to somewhere else where you can be free – go visit the nearest city or other major metropoles to hang out with like-minded friends and visit organic cafes. If you need to buy things, you'll be relying a lot on catalogues and websites, and even more so on a post-office box *in another town*.

Having said that – don't assume that you are as different as you think, *particularly* when it comes to sex. You'll find that residents of regional communities are doing it far more often than you would expect, simply because there isn't that much else to do!

Don't over-interpret
Alongside gossip comes the sin of over-interpretation. Someone does something for one reason, other people believe it was because of another reason, they get annoyed, suddenly everyone is making snide comments back and forth about how horrible they are, etc. Seems ridiculous? It is! But I've seen long-lasting friendships destroyed because of over-interpretation and an inability to stop and think for a moment.

What does this mean for you? Don't think too much about the actions of others, such as what exactly they said or why they didn't call at this particular time. It's possible they are doing it as part of a long-term project to crush your happiness and sense of belonging. Or they may have simply forgotten. One of these is far more likely than the other.

So in general – take a moment and relax. Be calm. Don't jump to conclusions. Nothing will bring you greater respect than being the level-headed one in a town full of fools.

7. Feeling lonely or bored

Moving to a new place is exciting – there are new things to see, secret locations to discover, new people to meet. But eventually the excitement will begin to wear off, the shiny veneer of the town will tarnish slightly, and you'll start to see the town for what it really is.

This is not a bad thing, of course, you cannot live somewhere without accepting it for what it is, but many new arrivals will begin to feel a sense of disappointment at this point. "I'm bored", they'll think, or "I feel lonely here". This is nothing to feel ashamed about, everyone has these thoughts, but it's important for your long-term happiness that you find the best way to beat these feelings.

In general, there are a few things which you should try to do in order to fight off these feelings

- Widen your circle of friends
- Take up a new hobby
- Get out of town for a bit

Let's look at these in a bit more detail.

Widen your circle of friends

Small towns are, well, small. Without many people. This means that the people who do live there will tend to pop up over and over again, you will run into acquaintances in all sorts of random locations – at the supermarket, the petrol station, walking in the surrounding hills. Everywhere, really.

This can be a problem – familiarity breeds contempt, as the old saying goes, because the more you see the same people the more you will find slight annoyances building up. If you aren't careful this can lead to dislike or even arguments, ruining a friendship and causing many problems in a small town where *everyone* will know what happened and which side they want to be on.

How do you avoid this? Make sure you don't always socialise with the same small group of friends. This is an easy habit to fall into, but you need to keep a wider social circle in order to remain balanced. In this sense friends are a lot like food – delicious, but best enjoyed in moderation.

Of course, this also means that you need to meet new people. We cover this in more detail in another chapter (see page 37), but it helps to have a set routine which brings you into contact with a wide variety of people. This may involve attending a church regularly, volunteering for a local society, even eating breakfast at a popular café every Sunday will bring you in contact with more people. The routine also helps reassure locals that you're a regular person, just like them (something which can be surprisingly difficult to prove sometimes!).

On the other hand, you have an automatic advantage from the moment you move into your new home. As a new resident, you will have a certain amount of novelty (quite a lot of novelty if it's a *really* small town) which will keep people interested in you and encourage them to come and chat. Try to hold on to this novelty for as long as possible – be sparing with what you reveal and drip-feed details about your past life over a longer period. This lets you ride the 'new and exciting' wave for as long as possible and brings you into contact with a wide range of potential friends.

Take up a new hobby

The best way to brighten up your life is to do something different, something fun to fill your time rather than just staring at the walls and wishing you were somewhere else. In other words, you need a hobby.

This is quite a broad thing to say, of course, there are hundreds of hobbies which you could take up and try out. The following section lists a couple which are well-suited to small-town lifestyles. Perhaps you might want to give them a try.

Active

- Go to the gym. Want to meet some like-minded people and get fit at the same time? Head over to the local gym. There's plenty of time to work out and you'll see the same faces on a regular basis. Just keep in mind that they're unlikely to have yoga or Pilates classes on offer.

- Go for a walk or jog around the neighbourhood. Everyone can work their way up to a level where they can run (they call it couch-to-5k for a reason) and there's no better way to learn about your new home while building up fitness than to go jogging.

- Go hiking or camping. Most of the time there'll be a forest, mountains, or hills in the area. Put on some sturdy shoes, maybe pack a tent, and then just go explore the surrounding nature. Just remember to get permission from the owners before crossing their fields and meadows, leave gates as you found them, and don't leave trash everywhere. Basic politeness, really.

- Living in a flat area or one with a lot of back-country tracks? There are plenty of opportunities to go quad-biking, horse-riding, motor-biking or more. Though not the cheapest of hobbies (especially horses), there are few better ways to get out in the sunshine and seeing the local sights.

Relaxed

- Read. There is a universe of literature out there, available both in physical form and as e-books. Why not take a bit of time out to relax in the sunshine and read a bit? Or take the chance and join a local book club, as a way to meet other reading fans?

- Feel like stretching your mind a bit? Why not try one of the many puzzles, crosswords and word-search books which are out there? (In particular those which the author may have written, for example on page 79!)

- Fan of cinema and TV? The spread of cable or streaming services such as Netflix means that you'll always have something to watch in the evenings when everything else is closed. Plus the size of a typical country home leaves plenty of space for a very nice home cinema set-up.

- If you're lucky your town will have their own cinema. Why not go and see a movie, even something which you normally wouldn't both with? Just be aware that you're unlikely to get the rarer foreign films or 'racy' options – that's what your home setup is for.

- Get a pet. The wide-open spaces and relaxed days are perfect for walking a dog, patting a cat, or planning out your ultimate aquarium. Pets help you to calm down after stressful days and will always be waiting for you when you get home.

- You have plenty of space, so why not use it to plant a really impressive garden? Regardless of whether you're into ornamental flowers or growing the largest pumpkins you can, gardening is a great way to spend some time outdoors without too much stress.

- Star-gazing. One of the amazing things about being outdoors at night in the countryside is just how *dark* it is. No lights as far as you can see, stars shining in a glorious black sky. If you've an interest in astronomy, then now is the chance to pick up a cheap telescope or pair of binoculars and look into the great beyond.

- Try your hand at fishing. Wild rivers, wide lakes and small streams – whatever your preferred fishing grounds, you're bound to find something interesting in a regional area. Relax on a sunny afternoon by yourself or with a few friends, and with luck you might even catch something.

Social

- Go to the local bars and restaurants. There aren't many options, that's true, but the regular meals will usually be done well and you're bound to run into an acquaintance or three. Just make sure you don't drink-drive on the way home, because news of your ticket will get around town in about 30 minutes, at most.

- Organise a party or dinner at your place. Whether it's a fancy three-course meal or a casual barbeque, you'll have no lack of visitors. Perfect for those who enjoy organising things, as even a mid-sized grill-fest can turn into a major project.

- Try out a board game evening. The world of board games has long since moved on from screaming family fights over Monopoly, there are now thousands of options for you to try which cater to every interest. Why not invite a few friends over and give it a go?

- Poker. It's a stereotype but it's true – there are few things better than having a couple of buddies over and whiling away the evening with a beer or three and a pack of cards.

Skill-up

- The internet has brought the world to our doorstep, knowledge about everything under the sun is now just a few clicks away. Whether you want to learn cross-stitch, programming, or car maintenance, there will be an online course of series of videos catering to your needs. So why not take the chance to improve your knowledge?

- Build up a side-hustle. As we just mentioned, you can learn pretty much anything in your spare time. Why not use that knowledge to build yourself a side hustle? From illustrating online to writing novels, you can learn something new and make a bit of extra income as well.

- Learn an instrument. There's no lack of instruments which you could pick up and start learning, from the classic guitar or piano through to an accordion or a Theremin. Plus the wide-open space between you and your neighbours will minimise any complaints while you're still…less than competent.

- Learn to cook. It is quite important to learn how to cook for yourself. Unlike major cities, small towns won't have much in the way of takeaway food or restaurants to visit. This means that if you want anything more than the 'standard meals', then you're going to have to make it yourself. Few things are worse than eating the same meal every single evening, which means it's up to you to bring something new to the table. Learn how to cook!

- Get artsy. Maybe you like sketching, or you've always wanted to try painting, or pottery-making seems like an interesting idea. Just give it a try. Many people in regional areas take up an artistic hobby on the side – you'll see evidence of it with every visit to friend's houses that you make.

Try anything

Is this all you can do? Not in the slightest, there are a million-and-one possible hobbies which you could take up, and a large chunk of those don't need a lot of other people or a hefty initial investment. Find something that interests you and give it a try – even if it's completely random, trying something new is the best way to entertain yourself and help break those depressed feelings.

Get out of town for a bit

Small town life can be great, but sometimes you just need to, well, get away. Out of town, off to a larger city, a different place, or an online space where you can recharge your energy and get away from the things which are irritating you.

Visit the city

We've mentioned many times that you need to embrace your new life in a small town or regional area. This is all well and good, but sometimes you're going to have longings for your old life and the things you used to enjoy. This is perfectly fine, everyone thinks like this. That's why most people take regular 'trips' to larger cities in order to catch up the life they left behind.

There are two main ways of doing this. One is to take semi-regular day-trips to the nearest city with the aim of collecting anything which might be lacking in your region. There are many things which you will only be able to get in a larger city – fancy food, unusual wine, different clothes, takeaway sushi, a suit, etc. You'll undoubtedly think of many of these as you go through your daily life, particularly just after you arrive in your new town. Keep a running list of what you need and try to organise everything in a day-trip. Make sure you spend a bit of time catching up on big-city lifestyle, both the good and the bad, to fulfil your cravings and (hopefully) remind yourself why you moved away.

The other approach is to take longer trips, holidays for a week or so, and go to visit a major metropole somewhere. You won't be doing your grocery shopping, but you can eat a hotdog in Manhattan, sing karaoke in Tokyo, or see an art gallery or three in London. This is a way to reset yourself, to enjoy a bit of time doing things which are simply not possible in a regional town, and so return home feeling a bit more refreshed.

Take a long holiday

The world is full of fantastic, beautiful places to visit, almost all of which are *not* in the small town which you are currently living in. Why not go and see one of them for a few weeks? Go lie on a beach in Asia, go skiing in the mountains of Colorado, drive a motorbike along the Italian coast. You are only limited by your imagination and budget, and a bit of clever planning will help you stretch your money much farther than you would expect.

Online booking portals have brought cheap holiday planning to everyone, no need to visit a travel agent. You undoubtedly have a bit of free time, so why not spend a weekend looking over options and deciding on your vacation? Even if you can't do it right away, the act of planning will help cheer you up and give you something to look forward to.

Escape online

If you can't manage to physically get out of town, then you can also look into getting out 'mentally'. Scattered across the internet are forums and groups devoted to every topic under the sun, from geo-political manoeuvring to caring for pet crocodiles. Whatever your interests, there will be others out there who want to discuss it. Why not go talk to them? Sign up for the forum, pick a username, and go chat about things which interest you. Ignore the fact that you may never see their faces or hear their voices, just the knowledge that others in the world share your topics can help to bring a bit of perspective to your current life.

Having said this, you need to actually have reliable internet access first, which can often be a challenge in regional areas. Take a bit of time to find a good internet provider, and get high speed internet if at all possible. This sounds a bit silly, but you will find yourself at home far more than you would if you were living in a city apartment, which means that you'll be needing some sort of entertainment. Even the most avid of outdoors types need to have some slack time in front of a screen at some stage, whether it be chatting on forums, watching streamed movies, or blasting away on a computer game – and this is where the internet connection comes in most handy.

Are you sure you want to live there?

It's possible that, even after trying all our suggestions, you aren't satisfied. The wider circle of acquaintances doesn't include anyone you would like to be friends with. The hobbies you've looked into don't really catch your eye, you can't find anyone who shares your interests. You're still lonely and bored.

It can even be more subtle than this. You may find that all of your weekends or holidays are spent 'escaping' to the city. Perhaps you never spend any time at home outside of sleeping. If this is the case, it may be a sign that you aren't actually happy where you are.

This is the point where you need to ask yourself what your true priorities and desires are. Do you really want to live in the town, or are you really dreaming of returning to the city? Would you rather the fresh air or the nearby café? There is no right or wrong answer here, everyone has their own feelings and needs to make their own choice. It can be an incredibly hard discussion to have, particularly if you have moved with others (such as your family) and they have different opinions.

But it is important to be honest with yourself. Look at the options and decide where you want to live. Because feeling out of place and unhappy in a small town can be a miserable experience.

Appendix: a checklist for moving

The actual process of moving to the countryside is a stressful one. You'll be packing everything up, getting ready for the move, unpacking a few boxes when you realise you need those shoes after all, repacking everything, running around frantically on the day of the move, and eating pizza on the floor in your new house.

Sounds familiar? Been there before? Here is a quick checklist with the most-important things to do during the move. It's certainly not exhaustive, so remember to add your own topics to it as well.

Two-three months before

This is the time to start planning out the big day! The major tasks you need to complete are:

- Sort your stuff and throw away things you don't want to keep (this takes much longer than you think, so plan accordingly)
- Budget for the move – how much can you afford to spend on movers and boxes?
- Contact moving companies for quotes
- If you'll be quitting your job, don't forget to give the required amount of notice.

One and a half months before

Moving day is getting closer, so you should start getting the administrative things in order:

- Get in touch with your doctor/dentist and get personal copies of your medical and dental records (both for you and your family members)

- Find out what medical/healthcare options are available in your new area and start picking out who you want to visit
- New house, new situation. Time to contact your insurance providers to discuss updates (and hopefully reduced payments) for your policies
- Cancel any memberships you may have in local groups and organizations – think gyms, delivery subscriptions, etc.
- Moving long-distance? Then make sure your travel arrangements are in place
- Order in all the moving supplies you'll need, such as boxes, tape and bubble wrap
- Remember those unwanted items from before? Now you should get rid of them – hold a garage sale, give them away to charity, take them to the tip
- If you have kids, contact your new schools and get the information you need for transferring their enrolment

One month before

Getting even closer now, so there's even more administrative things to do:

- Get in touch with your utility companies, you'll need to discontinue service on your move-out date and also set up new accounts in your new home. The major ones to keep in mind are:
    o Electricity
    o Water
    o Gas
    o Sewerage
    o Trash

- o   Telephone
- o   Cable and internet

- Booked the moving company? No? Then do it now! If you have already booked, then call to confirm your moving details with them
- Start the packing process, putting your rarely-used items into boxes.
- As you pack, keep a list of valuable items, in case you need to get insurance from the moving company
- I cannot overstate the importance of this one: *label boxes* as you pack
- Go to the local post office and fill out a change-of-address or post-forwarding form, so that lost letters can still catch up to you
- Notify any service or billing companies you are involved with of your move – think of credit cards, banks, etc.

Two weeks before

Things are getting really close now!

- Still working at your old job? Then schedule time off for your moving day. If you will be leaving, then hopefully you've given notice that you are quitting.
- Pack! Seriously!
- Will your new home need to be cleaned? If so, get this organised
- Start planning meals so that your fridge and pantry will be empty (or very close) by moving day. Few things are as frustrating as continuously packing the same can of tuna for multiple moves.

The week of your move

Less than a week until the big day!

- Finish your packing!
- But, make sure the essential things are in suitcases or bags rather than boxes, in case you need to get to them quickly
- Empty and defrost your refrigerator at least 24 hours before you move

Moving day

The big moving day rolls around! Hopefully you've followed the checklist and have organised most things beforehand. Despite that, you'll still find that there is stress, drama, and one or two things that you could have *sworn* you'd already done. But that's all part of the fun!

A last few things to keep in mind on the big day:

- If you've hired a company, then supervise and/or help them as they load the truck
- Make sure the important things get loaded last so that they can be unloaded first
- Check each room after it's been loaded to ensure you don't leave anything behind
- Do all of this in reverse at the new place
- Once everyone is gone, and the house is full of cardboard boxes, then you should be sure to enjoy a quiet fast-food dinner on the floor of your new home. Congratulations!

About the author

Arthur Kundell is a gardener, a farmer, and a huge fan of word searches. Having moved from the bustling city to a quiet town surrounded by farmland, he knows just how it feels to be the newcomer in a rural area. His published books build on his experiences as a gardener, as a 'new guy from the city', and as a word-search maniac.

The Real World Word Search series:

These word search puzzle books introduce readers to the words used by professionals and experts in the real world.

1. Farming
2. Tea and Coffee
3. Permaculture
4. Ecology
5. Chemistry
6. Geology
7. Physics
8. Astronomy
9. Space & Rocketry
10. Dinosaurs
11. Aussie Slang
12. 1920s Slang
13. Quite Tricky
14. 1960s Slang
15. Cars
16. Cooking
17. Christmas
18. Middle Ages
19. Knights
20. Cowboys
21. Wild West Slang
22. Pirates
23. Investing
24. Soccer
25. Cricket
26. Baseball

Available in print from Amazon and other retailers.

Coffee and your garden

Available as an eBook and Print version

Disappointed by the amount of waste in the coffee industry, Arthur decided to introduce people to the wonders of coffee grounds. His book covers their many uses in your garden.

Getting Away: a simple guide to moving to the countryside

Available as an eBook and Print version

Tired of the city life and looking for something greener, quieter, more relaxed? This book covers the process of moving from the city to the countryside.

Printed in Great Britain
by Amazon